This Book Belongs to:

TO: BEU

God Bless,
Sandra Maldner
Jer. 29:11

PEg. 9652
Psalm 102:18

This book is dedicated to the memory of my loving daughter,
Tiffany, who inspired it.

When Tiffany was little, we found a cute stuffed frog on a paper lily pad
with the words, "Fully Reliant On God." From that moment on, whenever
we used the word "frog," we understood its real meaning.

Through this story, I pray that Tiffany and Forest will live on in
the hearts and minds of children everywhere as they await their own
"crown of rye chestnuts."

Tiffany is wearing hers already.

Tiffany Marie Frank
April 5, 1978 – January 20, 2003

"And now the prize awaits me—the crown of righteousness, which the Lord,
the righteous Judge, will give me on the day of his return. And the prize is
not just for me, but for all who eagerly look forward to his appearing."

2 Timothy 4:8

ISBN 978-0-615-24821-9

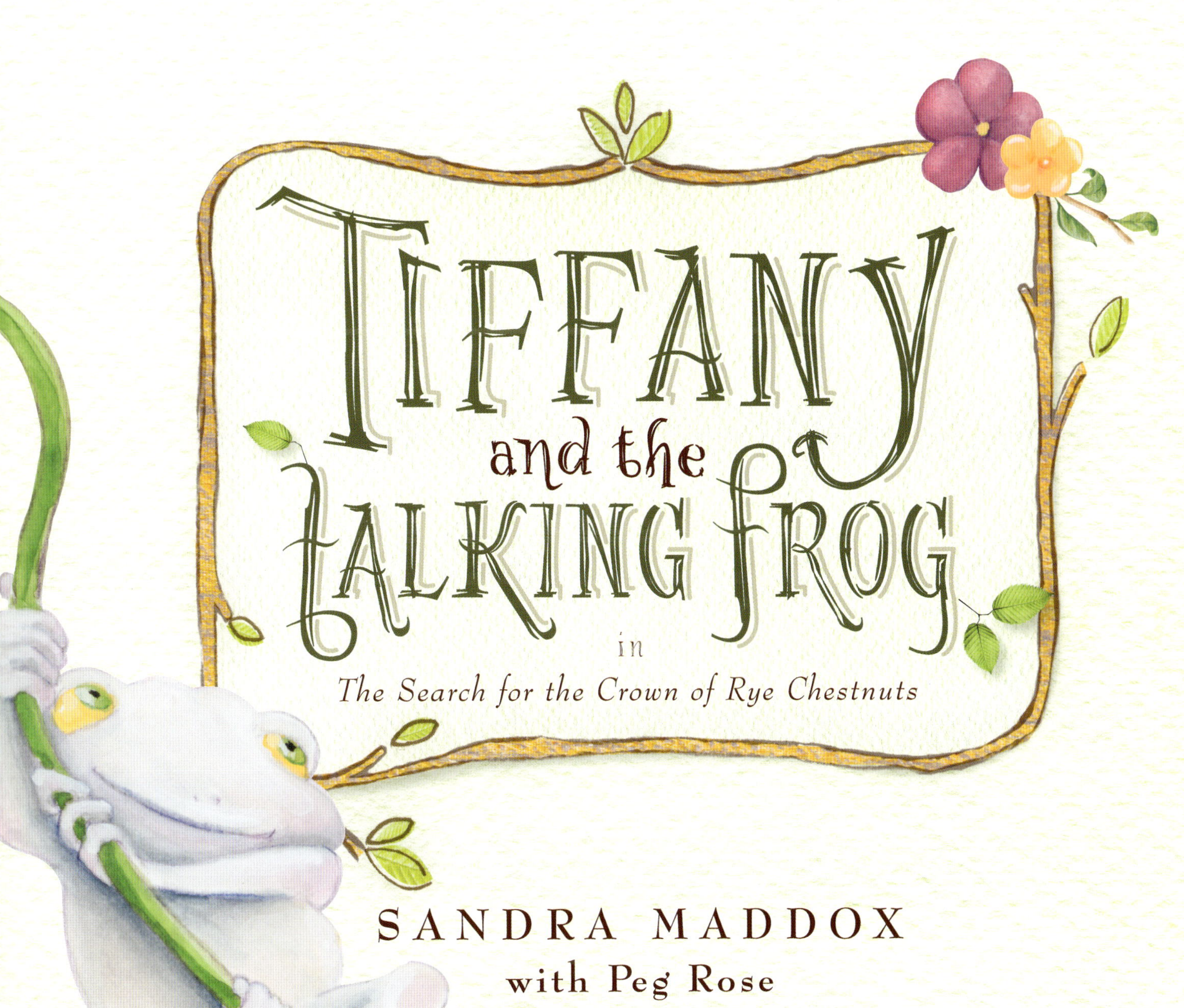

Tiffany and the Talking Frog

in

The Search for the Crown of Rye Chestnuts

SANDRA MADDOX

with Peg Rose

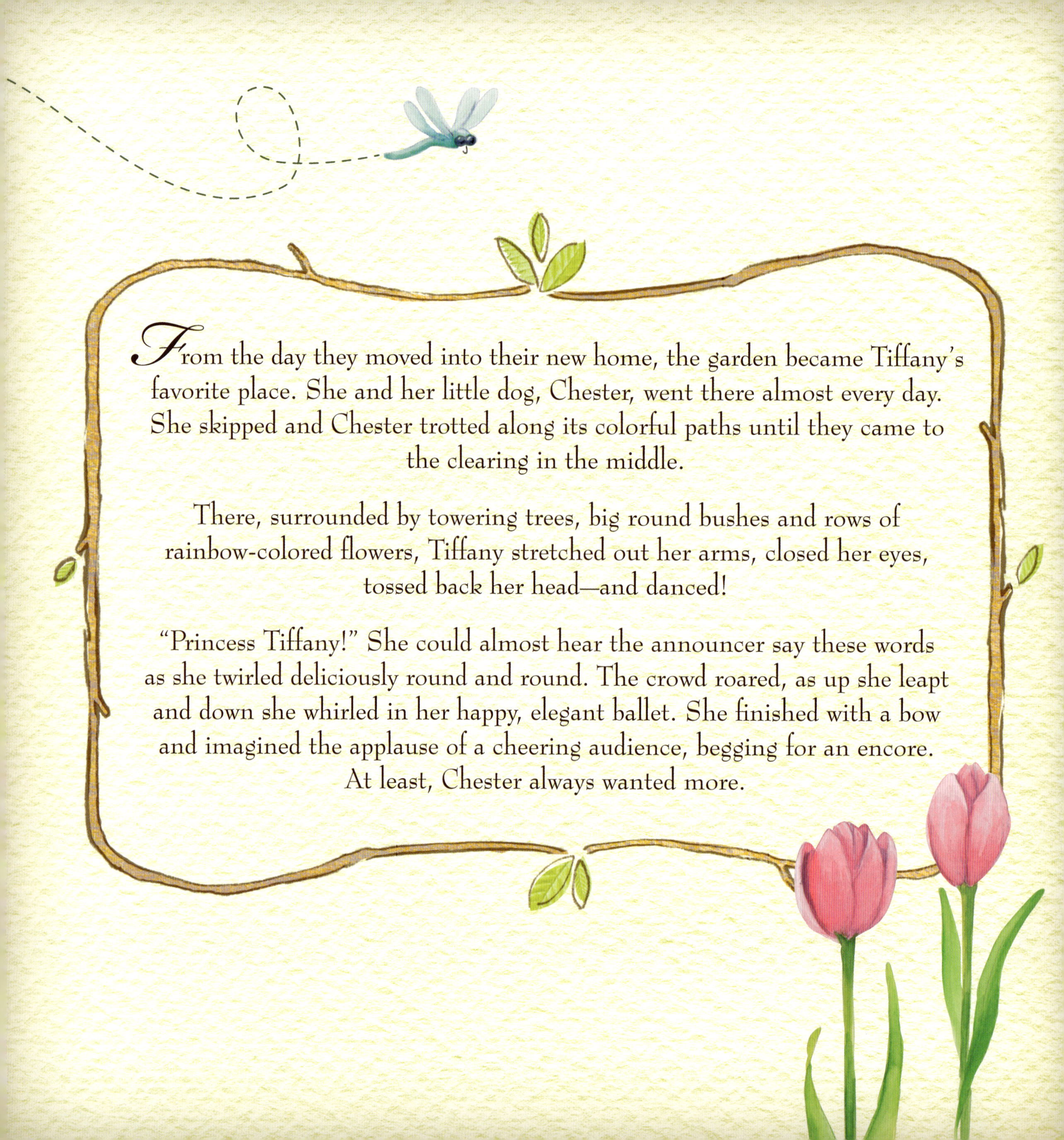

From the day they moved into their new home, the garden became Tiffany's favorite place. She and her little dog, Chester, went there almost every day. She skipped and Chester trotted along its colorful paths until they came to the clearing in the middle.

There, surrounded by towering trees, big round bushes and rows of rainbow-colored flowers, Tiffany stretched out her arms, closed her eyes, tossed back her head—and danced!

"Princess Tiffany!" She could almost hear the announcer say these words as she twirled deliciously round and round. The crowd roared, as up she leapt and down she whirled in her happy, elegant ballet. She finished with a bow and imagined the applause of a cheering audience, begging for an encore. At least, Chester always wanted more.

But today, Tiffany heard a different noise. "What's that?" she asked Chester, who just tilted his head and lifted an ear. Whatever it was, it definitely did NOT sound like applause.

"Ribbit, ribbit, ri-hi-hi-hi-hibbit, ri-hi-hi-hi-hi-hibbit. Oh, ri-hi-hi-hi-hi-hi-hi-hibbit… awwwwwwww-bit!"

Turning from their imaginary audience, Tiffany and Chester followed the ri-hi-hi-hi-hibbits into the bushes. When the sound stopped, Tiffany stopped and listened. Then she heard it—the unmistakable sound of sniffling. She'd done enough of that in her life to know what sniffling sounded like.

$\mathcal{P}$arting the leaves that had grown over a pond, Tiffany rubbed
her eyes and stared—there before her sat a little white frog on a lily pad,
sobbing his heart out. He was so absorbed in his own pity party, he
had not heard Tiffany and Chester approach. When she spoke,
her voice sent him leapfrogging ten feet high!

"Ooohh, why are you crying, little frog?" Tiffany asked. Of course,
Tiffany didn't expect an answer. She knew animals didn't talk, at least,
not in real life. Maybe in storybooks and cartoons, but not really.
She and Chester understood each other—but kids and dogs always do.
"I didn't mean to scare you," she said softly, hoping to soothe the frog,
"I just wondered what's making you so sad."

"Can't you see?" snapped the frog after he'd landed and regained his
balance. His voice was thick and snuffly from crying.

A talking frog? Tiffany thought. No, it couldn't be. Still… she
looked around her to make sure no one was watching… and then she
answered—just in case this really was a talking frog.

"See what?"

"In case you didn't know," said the frog with mounting impatience,
"frogs are s'posed to be green!" Using his front leg, he gestured to his
own pale body. "And obviously, I'm not!"

"Oh!" said Tiffany. "Is that all?"

"Is that all? Isn't it enough?"

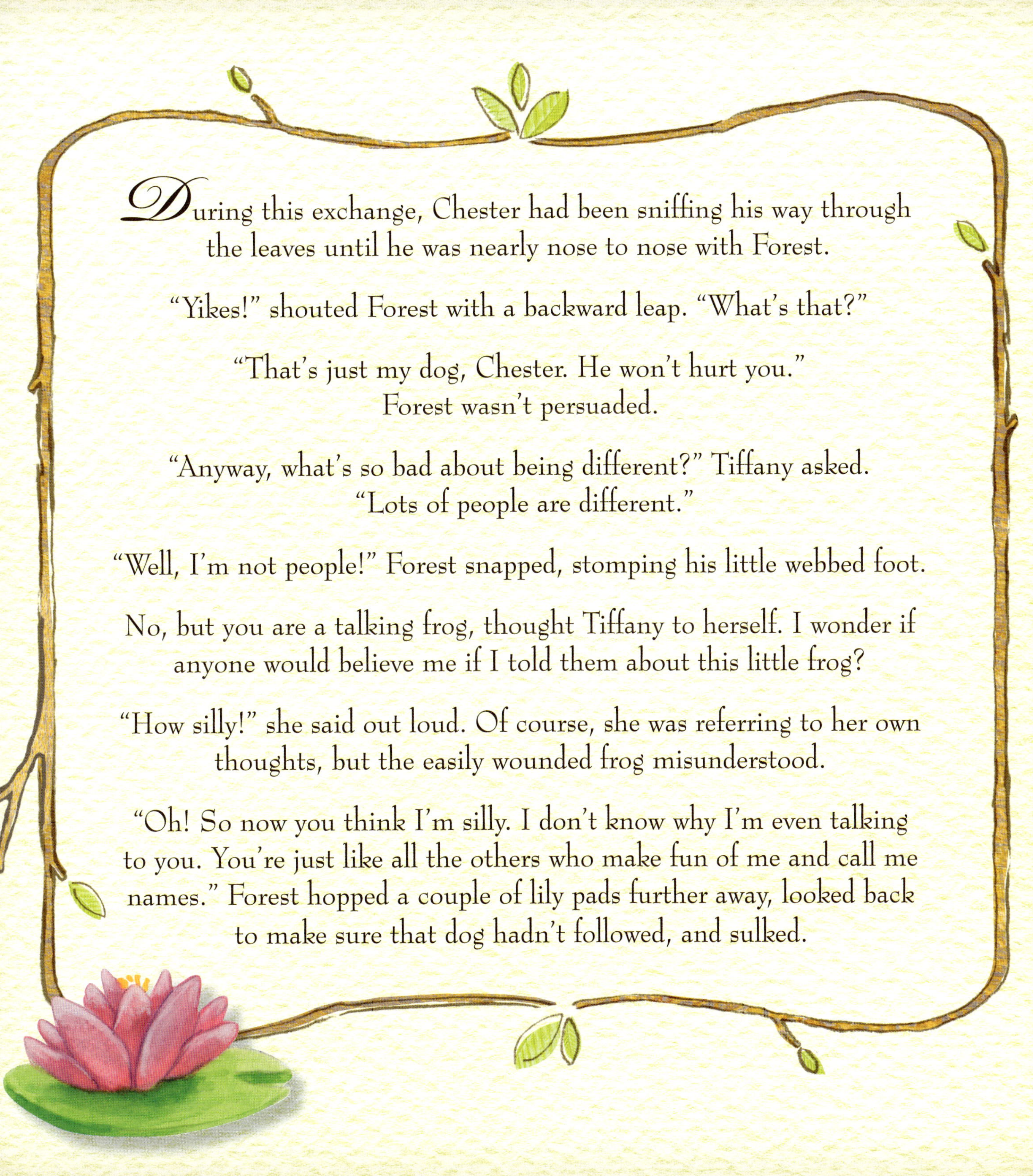

$\mathcal{D}$uring this exchange, Chester had been sniffing his way through the leaves until he was nearly nose to nose with Forest.

"Yikes!" shouted Forest with a backward leap. "What's that?"

"That's just my dog, Chester. He won't hurt you."
Forest wasn't persuaded.

"Anyway, what's so bad about being different?" Tiffany asked.
"Lots of people are different."

"Well, I'm not people!" Forest snapped, stomping his little webbed foot.

No, but you are a talking frog, thought Tiffany to herself. I wonder if anyone would believe me if I told them about this little frog?

"How silly!" she said out loud. Of course, she was referring to her own thoughts, but the easily wounded frog misunderstood.

"Oh! So now you think I'm silly. I don't know why I'm even talking to you. You're just like all the others who make fun of me and call me names." Forest hopped a couple of lily pads further away, looked back to make sure that dog hadn't followed, and sulked.

Tiffany sat down on a large boulder next to the pond. Her thick brown pig tails fell forward as she planted her chin on her fist, elbows resting on her knees. Whenever she had a lot on her mind, she put her three middle fingers in her mouth. Somehow, it helped her concentrate.

What can I do to cheer up this sulky frog? Tiffany thought.

Pulling her fingers out, she said, "Speaking of names, mine's Tiffany. What's yours?"

"Forest," said the frog. "My mom named me that. She hoped it would make me turn green. It didn't work."

"Okay Forest," said Tiffany, "you still haven't told me what's so bad about being a white frog."

"What's so bad? Nobody else will play with me, that's what!" Forest said. "None of the other frogs will catch flies with me, or swim with me, or even share a lily pad with me. They treat me like I'm not even there!"

"Gosh," said Tiffany, "I'm sorry. That must be hard. I bet you're lonely, huh?"

"I don't know why I was ever born!" Forest railed, unable to hear anyone but himself.

Tiffany stuck her fingers back in her mouth and pondered Forest's problem.

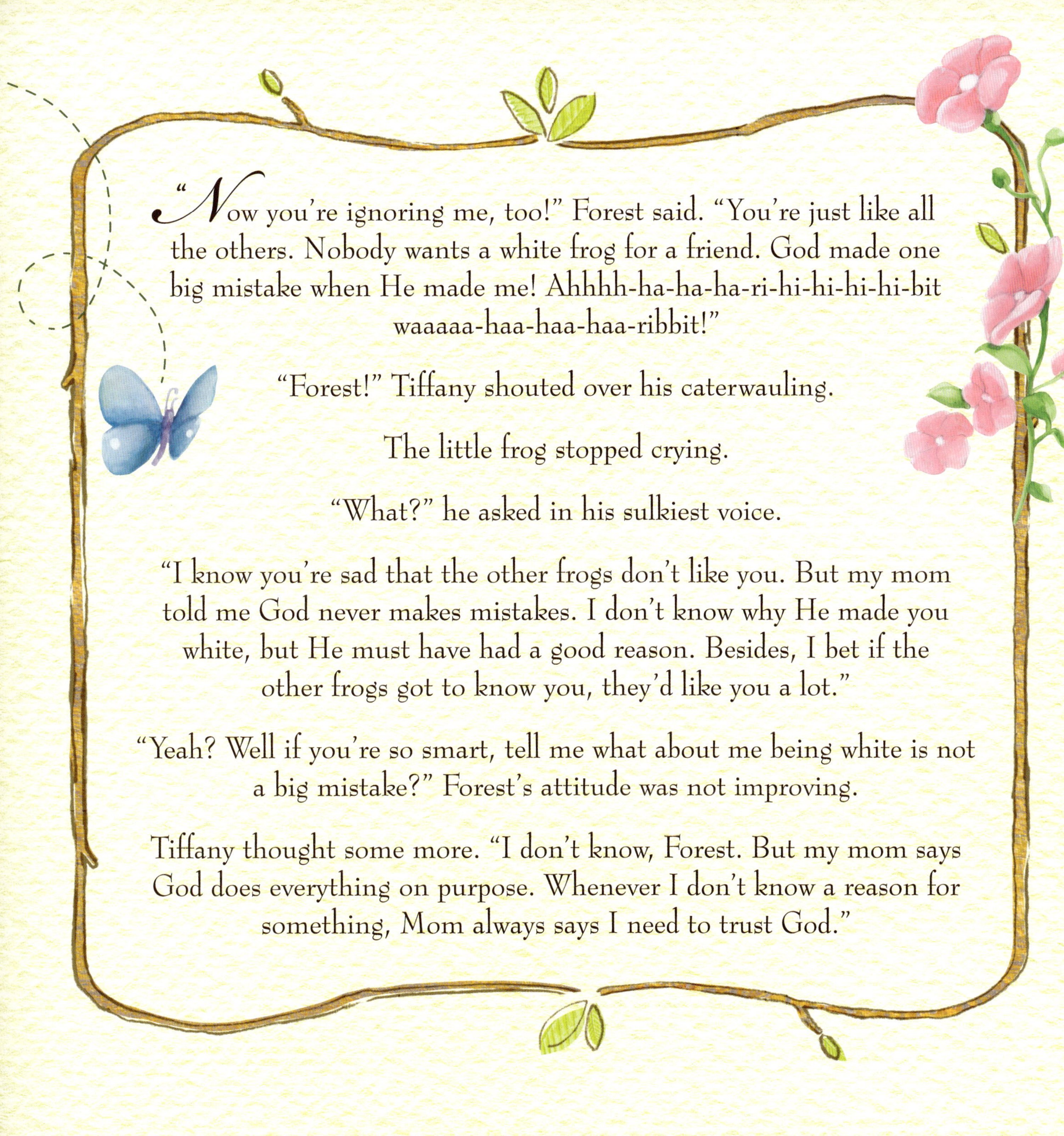

"*N*ow you're ignoring me, too!" Forest said. "You're just like all the others. Nobody wants a white frog for a friend. God made one big mistake when He made me! Ahhhh-ha-ha-ha-ri-hi-hi-hi-hi-bit waaaaa-haa-haa-haa-ribbit!"

"Forest!" Tiffany shouted over his caterwauling.

The little frog stopped crying.

"What?" he asked in his sulkiest voice.

"I know you're sad that the other frogs don't like you. But my mom told me God never makes mistakes. I don't know why He made you white, but He must have had a good reason. Besides, I bet if the other frogs got to know you, they'd like you a lot."

"Yeah? Well if you're so smart, tell me what about me being white is not a big mistake?" Forest's attitude was not improving.

Tiffany thought some more. "I don't know, Forest. But my mom says God does everything on purpose. Whenever I don't know a reason for something, Mom always says I need to trust God."

Forest started to say something, but caught a fly with his tongue instead.

"Hey!" Tiffany shouted, suddenly remembering something wonderful. "You're a F.R.O.G.!"

"Of course I'm a frog!" snapped Forest impatiently.

"Don't you know frogs are God's reminders? F.R.O.G. stands for Fully Reliant On God!" said Tiffany.

"And where did you get that bright idea?" Forest grumbled.

"My…"

"Wait! Don't tell me. Your mom."

"How did you know?" Tiffany said.

Forest turned his back on Tiffany and thought about sulking some more. He also thought about what she had said. Hmmm, Fully Reliant On God. That's not such a bad thing to stand for. I wonder if the other frogs know that?

"Well Forest, I know one reason God made you the way you are. He made you to be my friend! I've never had a talking frog for a friend before."

"Your friend?" said Forest. "You mean it?"

"Of course, I do, sil…" Tiffany almost said "silly," but then she remembered how that word made Forest cry before, and she didn't want that to happen again!

"Yes, I'd really like it if we could be friends. Chester, too!"

Chester yipped in agreement.

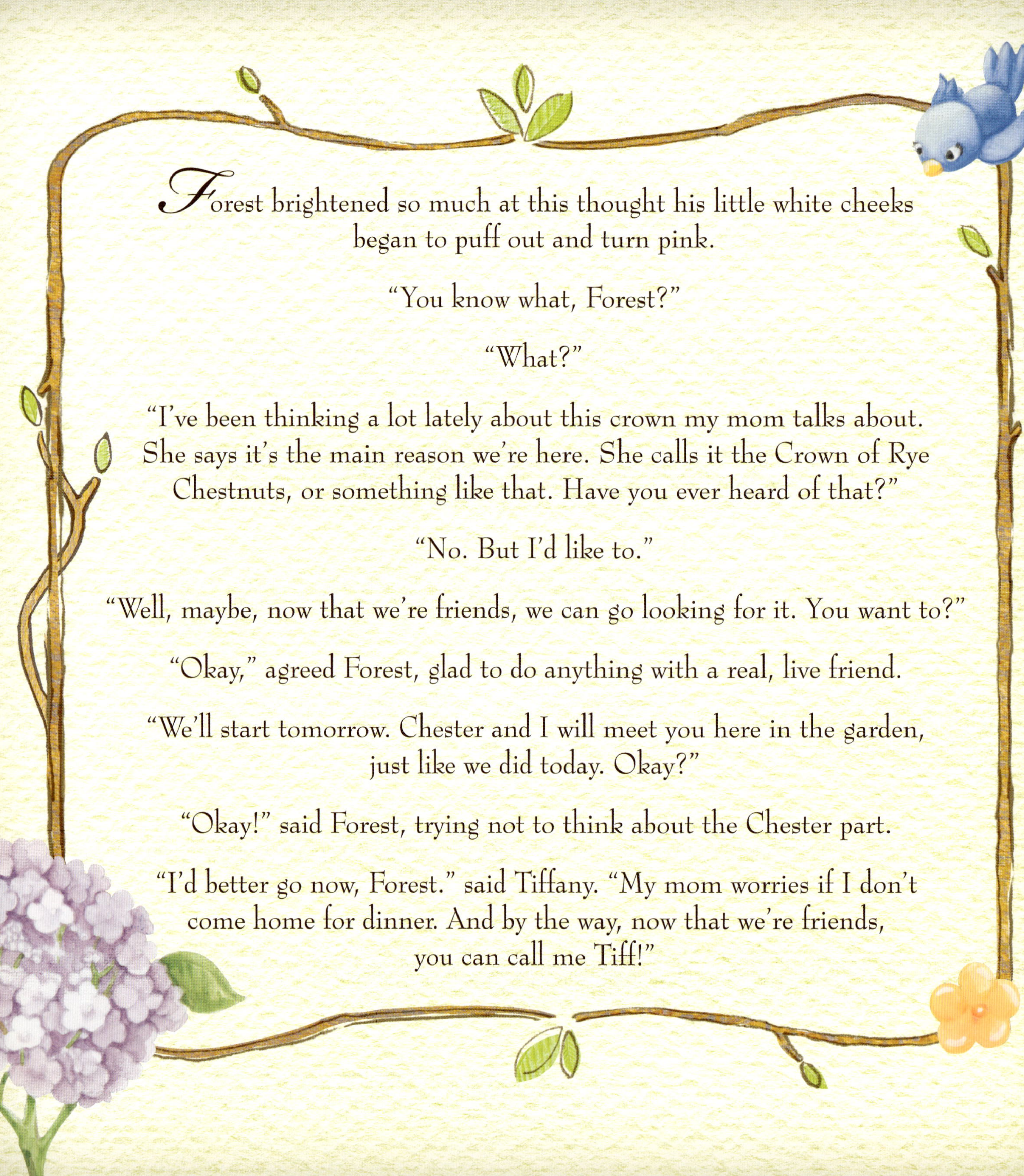

Forest brightened so much at this thought his little white cheeks began to puff out and turn pink.

"You know what, Forest?"

"What?"

"I've been thinking a lot lately about this crown my mom talks about. She says it's the main reason we're here. She calls it the Crown of Rye Chestnuts, or something like that. Have you ever heard of that?"

"No. But I'd like to."

"Well, maybe, now that we're friends, we can go looking for it. You want to?"

"Okay," agreed Forest, glad to do anything with a real, live friend.

"We'll start tomorrow. Chester and I will meet you here in the garden, just like we did today. Okay?"

"Okay!" said Forest, trying not to think about the Chester part.

"I'd better go now, Forest." said Tiffany. "My mom worries if I don't come home for dinner. And by the way, now that we're friends, you can call me Tiff!"

Forest thought about his new friend Tiff and the Crown of Rye Chestnuts.

Wow, he thought, a friend and an adventure, too—all in the same day.
Life was beginning to look a lot better.

Tiffany looked up and noticed the day had slipped away from her. The sky
had grown dark. It was much later than dinner time!

"Wow, Forest," said Tiffany, looking around her. "It's getting dark out!
I've never been in the garden this late before. I don't think I can see my
way out. What am I going to do? My mom is probably getting worried."

$\mathcal{T}$hey were quiet for awhile, thinking some more.

"Tiff?" said Forest.

"Yes?" Tiffany answered.

"Can you see me?" Forest asked.

"Sure I can see you. Why?"

"Well," said Forest, "maybe if I hop in front of you I can kind of mark the path to help you find your way home."

"Oh, Forest!" Tiffany said. "I think that might work! But what about you? How will you get back to the pond?"

"Oh, a frog can always find his way back to water," said Forest. Secretly, he had no idea if he'd be able to find his way back. He'd never been more than a lily pad or two from home before in his life. Bravely, for Tiffany, Forest ventured out into the garden and down its path. Hop. Hop-hop. Hop. With each leap, he rested a moment and made sure Tiffany and Chester were following. Hop. Hop-hop-hop. Hop.

"Forest, I can see my house!" Tiffany said.

"Tiffany! Where are you?" There was her mom calling her name.
"I'm here, Mom! I'm coming!" Before she turned to run home, Tiffany
bent down and scooped Forest into her hands. "Thank you, Forest, for
helping me find my way home. I'm always going to think of you whenever
I get scared from now on. You are so brave."

Forest beamed.

"And you know what else?" Tiffany said.

Forest raised his little eyebrows. "What?" he said.

"If God hadn't made you white, you wouldn't have been able to help me
find my way home in the dark."

"Oh!" Forest said.

Just then a thunder-clap rolled and a lightning strike split the sky.

"Forest!" Tiffany shouted.

"What?" Forest said again.

"For a minute there, in the lightning, I could almost see a crown on your head."

"Really?"

"Well, maybe it just looked like it, 'cause I don't see it now.
But I was sure it was a crown."

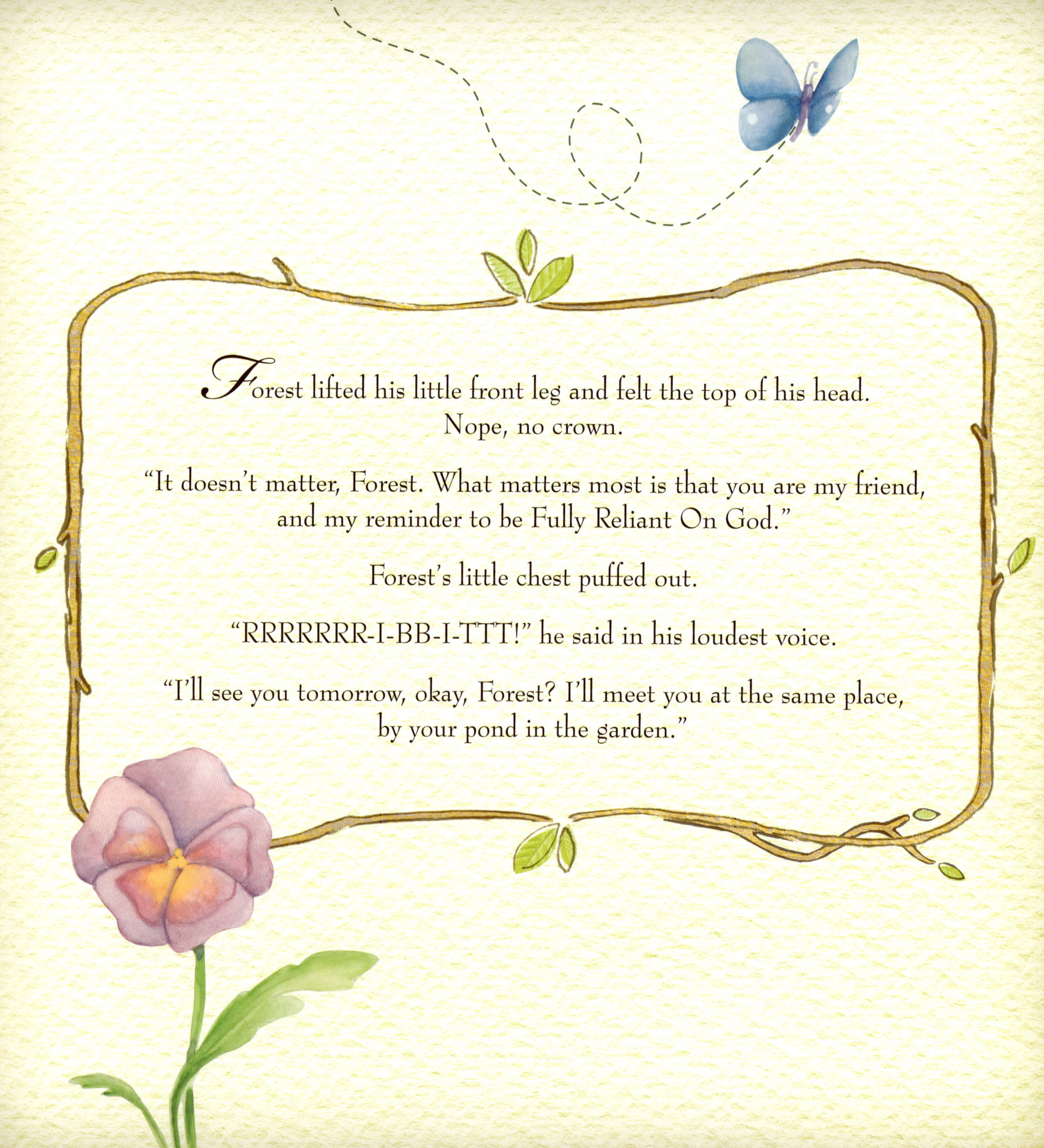

Forest lifted his little front leg and felt the top of his head.
Nope, no crown.

"It doesn't matter, Forest. What matters most is that you are my friend,
and my reminder to be Fully Reliant On God."

Forest's little chest puffed out.

"RRRRRRR-I-BB-I-TTT!" he said in his loudest voice.

"I'll see you tomorrow, okay, Forest? I'll meet you at the same place,
by your pond in the garden."

$\mathcal{T}$iffany ran home and Forest hopped back toward the garden.
As the big raindrops pelted him, he thought God, if you're really there,
I hope you can help me find my way home.

"Forest," he heard a voice say, "trust me."

God? thought Forest. No, it couldn't be. Still…

He looked around to make sure no one was watching… and then
he answered—just in case this really was God.

"Is it really you?" Forest asked.

And he followed the voice that led him all the way home.

THE END

Acknowledgements

A heartfelt thanks to my dear friend Peg Rose, who made the words on these pages come to life… she is the world's best wordsmith!

Thank you to the unparalleled team at David Riley Associates.

Especially to David and Yvonne Riley whose hearts are united in pain with ours over the tragic loss of our daughters.

Special thanks to my family, my sweet father-in-law David, my mom Olga, my siblings Patricia, Annette, Hector, Michelle and my niece Natty for your support, encouragement and love… I love you all.

But most of all… I want to thank Ron, my husband, my best friend and biggest cheerleader. Thank you for loving me… you helped this book (and this author) in more ways than you will ever know.
I am in love with you.

About the AUTHOR

Sandra Maddox is a wife, mom, gifted interior designer and active member of her church community. At Saddleback Church in Lake Forest, California, Sandra is the coordinator for Treasured, an outreach ministry for moms with pre-schoolers. When Sandra is not volunteering her time in various ministries, she is spending time with her husband Ron and their two dogs in Newport Beach, CA.